10/97

PRZEWALSKI'S HORSE

by Charlotte Wilcox

Reading Consultant:
Tony Fisher
Minnesota Zoo

C A P S T O N E P R E S S
M A N K A T O , M I N N E S O T A

C A P S T O N E   P R E S S
818 North Willow Street • Mankato, Minnesota 56001

Printed in the United States of America.

Library of Congress Cataloging-in-Publication Data
Wilcox, Charlotte.
    Przewalski's horse/by Charlotte Wilcox
    p. cm. -- (Learning about horses)
    Includes bibliographical references (p. 45) and index.
    Summary: Discusses the last truly wild equine species, which has been
    extinct in the wild since the 1960s but was recently reintroduced into its
    native habitat in Mongolia.
    ISBN 1-56065-466-X
    1. Przewalski's horses--Juvenile literature. [1. Przewalski's horse.
2. Horses.] I. Title. II. Series.
SF363.W55 1997
599.665'5--dc21

                      96-47696
                      CIP
                      AC

Photo credits
Michael Francis, cover, 12, 22, 41, 42
FPG, 16, 32; Chris Michaels, 6; Jonathan Meyers, 8; Stan
    Osolinski, 14; Robin Smith, 34
James Rowan, 10, 30, 38-39
William Muñoz, 18
Visuals Unlimited/Barry Pribula, 25; Kjell B. Sandred, 36
Unicorn/Phyllis Kedl, 26
Foundation for the Preservation and Protection of the
    Przewalski's Horse, 28

Table of Contents

Quick Facts about Przewalski's Horse 4

Chapter 1 The Last Wild Horse 7

Chapter 2 Not Like Other Horses 11

Chapter 3 Living on the Steppe 17

Chapter 4 Capturing Przewalski's Horses 23

Chapter 5 Zoos to the Rescue 31

Chapter 6 Back to the Wild 35

Photo Diagram 38

Words to Know 44

To Learn More 45

Useful Addresses 46

Internet Sites 46

Where to See Przewalski's Horses 47

Index 48

Quick Facts about Przewalski's (Prihz-VAHL-skeez) Horse

Description

Height: Males stand 54 to 58 inches (138 to 146 centimeters) tall. Females stand 48 to 55 inches (120 to 140 centimeters) tall. Their height is measured from the ground to the top of the shoulders.

Weight: A full-grown Przewalski's horse weighs from 550 to 850 pounds (247 to 383 kilograms).

Physical features: Przewalski's horse is a separate species from other horses. A species is any group of living things with common characteristics. Przewalski's horse has a thick neck and a straight back. The head is shorter than the heads of tame horses. The mane stands straight up instead of falling to the side.

Color: The coat is a tan color called dun. The under part of the coat is lighter than the top. The legs, mane, and tail are dark brown or black. A dark brown stripe runs along the backbone.

Development

History of
breed: Przewalski's horses are the last
                descendants of an ancient horse species.
                None could be found in the wild after
                1970.

Place of origin: In ancient times, these animals roamed
                across Europe and Asia. Their last range
                area was in central Asia.

Numbers: More than 1,000 Przewalski's horses
                now live in about 130 zoos worldwide.
                About 200 have been returned to the
                wild in Mongolia (Mahn-GO-lee-ah).

Life History

Life span: A healthy Przewalski's horse may live
                20 to 30 years in a zoo. In the wild,
                their life span may be shorter.

Uses

Przewalski's horse is a wild, endangered species.
Endangered means in danger of no longer existing.
Przewalski's horses live in zoos or wildlife parks. They
are not trained to ride.

Chapter 1

The Last Wild Horse

In caves near Lascaux (Lahs-COE), France, there are many animal pictures painted on the smooth walls. There are hundreds of pictures of horses, deer, cattle, bison, and lions. It is believed that these pictures were made by ancient people.

There are many other painted caves in that region. Similar painted caves are in Italy and Spain. The pictures are thousands of years old.

The cave pictures have lasted longer than some of the animals they show. Some of the painted animals are now extinct. Extinct means they no longer exist. Other animals shown on the walls have changed over time.

The Przewalski's horse looks like cave paintings made thousands of years ago.

Figures similar to Przewalski's horses were found on painted cave walls.

The cave horses do not look exactly like today's riding or working horses. But they do look very much like Przewalski's horses.

Written Records

Przewalski's horses were first written about 1,000 years ago. A monk from Tibet (Tih-BEHT) wrote about them. A Mongolian wrote about them 300 years later. The Mongolion writer told how a herd of wild horses ran in front of the famous Mongolian emperor Genghis Khan (JENG-gus KAHN). The wild horses frightened the emperor's horse. The emperor's horse reared and threw him to the ground.

Another Mongolian history book tells how valuable the wild horses were. In 1630, the emperor of Mongolia gave one to the emperor of Manchuria (Man-CHUR-ee-ah). It was a very fine gift.

In 1750, the emperor of Manchuria organized a great hunt. He and his warriors killed more than 200 Przewalski's horses in one day. They hunted the horses for meat. They made leather out of the skins.

Przewalski's horses are also called Asian wild horses. They once galloped across most of Europe and Asia. Today there are only about 1,300 Przewalski's horses left in the world. Only a few of them run free in their native home. The rest live in zoos and wildlife parks.

Chapter 2

Not Like Other Horses

Przewalski's horses are not the same species as domestic horses. Domestic horses have been raised, tamed, and used by humans for thousands of years. Przewalski's horses do not look or act like domestic horses. But both animals are part of a larger group called equines (EE-kwines). The equine animal group includes horses, donkeys, and zebras.

All domestic horse breeds enjoy kind and gentle human attention. Even mustangs captured from the wild learn to love their owners. But Przewalski's horses never learn to love people. They can become tame, but they are difficult to train. They can sometimes be mean to those who take care of them.

Przewalski's horses can become tame, but they are difficult to train.

Przewalski's horses have dun-colored coats and dark manes and tails.

Coloring

All Przewalski's horses are the same color. They are a tan color called dun. The head and neck are a darker shade than the body. The coat on the under part of the body is a light cream color. The lower part of the face and rings around the eyes are light cream or even white.

The legs, mane, and tail are dark brown or black. In the winter, the coat turns light tan to almost white. In the summer, the coat grows darker.

Przewalski's horses have unique markings. Their legs often have stripes around them like a zebra's. A dark brown stripe runs along the backbone. This is called a dorsal (DOHR-sul) stripe. Some domestic horses also have a dorsal stripe.

Some Przewalski's horses have another stripe coming down from the withers. The withers is the spot at the top of the horse's shoulders. The stripe may be on one side or both sides of the shoulder. Donkeys sometimes have this cross stripe, too.

Hair, Mane, and Tail

The hair at the top of a Przewalski's horse's tail is much shorter than other horses. The longer hairs start farther down on the tail. Przewalski's horses grow new manes and tails every year. This does not happen to other horses.

The Przewalski's horse's mane stands straight up on the neck. On other horses, the mane falls softly to the side of the neck. Most domestic horses have bangs in front. The bangs are called

the forelock. Przewalski's horses do not have a forelock.

Size

Przewalski's horses are smaller than average riding horses. Adult males stand 54 to 58 inches (138 to 146 centimeters) tall from the ground to the withers. Adult females stand 48 to 55 inches (120 to 140 centimeters) tall. A full-grown Przewalski's horse weighs 550 to 850 pounds (247 to 383 kilograms).

The Przewalski's horse's head is also different from domestic horses. It is larger in comparison to its body and has a rounder shape. The eyes are set closer together and higher on the head. The top lip sticks out a little farther than the bottom lip.

The Przewalski's horse's back is not like other horses. The domestic horse's back dips down in the middle. This makes it a nice animal to ride. But a Przewalski's horse has a straight back like a zebra. This type of back is not suitable for riding.

Like a zebra, Przewalski's horses have a straight back unsuitable for riding.

Chapter 3

Living on the Steppe

Przewalski's horses have always lived on the steppe (STEHP). This is a large area of grassland in the Eastern Hemisphere. The Eastern Hemisphere is the half of the world east of the Atlantic Ocean. The steppe stretches for thousands of miles across central Europe and Asia. It is similar to the prairie of North America.

Few trees grow on the steppe. The land is mostly flat and covered with grass. Some areas can be dry, but there are rivers. This land is perfect for large, hooved animals that eat grass.

In ancient times, herds of wild horses thundered across the steppe. They shared their home with antelope, bison, and cattle. There was plenty of grass for all of them.

Przewalski's horses have always lived on the steppe.

The Shrinking Steppe

Over many centuries, the steppe began to shrink. Land that once had just a few trees became forests. Places that were dry became deserts. Forests and deserts do not grow much grass.

People living on the steppe began raising more domestic cattle, sheep, and horses. The domestic animals were well cared for. They had the best grass and water supplies. The wild animals moved toward the mountain and desert areas. Their herds became smaller because there was less to eat.

The wild horse was no longer master of the steppe. Male horses called stallions led their herds far away from people and domestic animals. They became shy creatures seen only by hunters and explorers.

The wild horses finally disappeared from Europe completely. Few people in Europe even remembered they had been there. But a man named Nikolai Przewalski (NICK-oh-lie Prihz-VAHL-skee) remembered.

Przewalski's horses began to disappear when the steppe began to shrink.

19

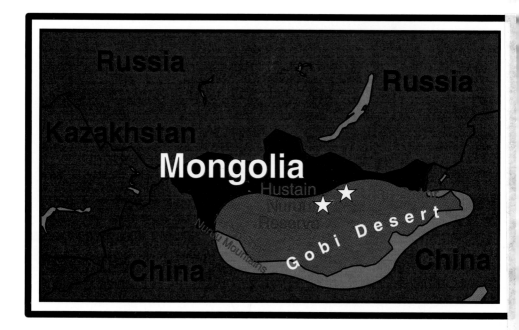

Przewalski's Discovery

Nikolai Przewalski was born in 1839. He became an officer in the Russian army. Przewalski was an expert in surveying land to draw maps. He explored many out-of-the-way places in Asia.

In 1879, Przewalski traveled to Mongolia. He explored and mapped the Takhin Shar

Nuruu (Tahk-HEEN Shahr New-RUE) region. This name means "yellow mountains of the wild horse" in Mongolian. This area is on the northern edge of the Gobi (GOH-bee) Desert.

When Przewalski was leaving Mongolia, someone gave him a wild horse's skull and tan-colored hide. The local people called the wild horses takhi (TAH-kee). This means "spirit" in their language.

Przewalski wondered about the gift. At first, he did not believe it was really a wild horse. When he returned to Russia, Przewalski brought the skull and hide to the Academy of Science in St. Petersburg.

At the academy, Dr. I.S. Poliakov (Poh-lee-ACK-of) studied the skull and hide. He found that they did belong to a wild horse. Dr. Poliakov named the new species after the man who showed it to him. People have called the wild horses Przewalski's horses ever since.

Chapter 4

Capturing
Przewalski's Horses

Nikolai Przewalski returned to Mongolia in 1880. This time, he found two herds of wild horses. He wrote down what they looked like and how they acted. He tried to hunt them, but he was not successful. He said they were very afraid of humans and could run fast.

On the Hunt

In 1889, the Russian army sent two officers to explore western China. Like Przewalski, they drew maps and studied the lands they explored. The two officers were brothers named Grigory and Mikhail Grum-Grzhimailo (GRIHG-or-ee and Mick-HI-uhl Groom-GRIHZ-ee-my-loh).

Wild Przewalski's horses are afraid of humans.

The brothers were better hunters than Przewalski. They tracked a herd of wild horses for several days. They shot three stallions and a female horse called a mare. The brothers sent the skins and some bones from the horses to the academy in St. Petersburg.

The reports from Przewalski and the Grum-Grzhimailo brothers puzzled scientists. Many did not believe a separate wild horse species existed. Soon people made plans to catch some. This would settle the question.

Planning a Capture

Two German scientists planned the first capture. Their names were D.A. Clemenz (Clem-MENZ) and C.E. Büchner (BEWK-ner). They teamed up with Nikolai Assanov (NICK-oh-lie AH-sen-of). Assanov was a Russian who lived in Mongolia. Together the men made a plan. But they did not have enough money to carry it out.

The three men approached a rich German named Friederich von Falz-Fein (FREED-rick VON FAHLTZ-FINE). He owned a large estate called Askania Nova (Ahs-KAHN-ee-ah NOH-vah) in southern Ukraine. Falz-Fein had half a million sheep on his estate. He also raised cattle and horses.

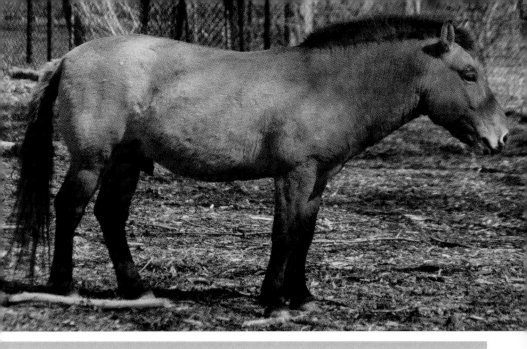

In the 1800s, many scientists did not believe a separate wild horse species existed.

Falz-Fein was interested in rare animals. He liked the idea of bringing some Przewalski's horses to his estate. Falz-Fein agreed to pay for the capture. The plan went into action.

Asian Roundup

Assanov hired Russian and Mongolian hunters to help with the capture. Nobody thought they could take a full-grown Przewalski's horse alive. The adult horses were too fast and very afraid of humans. They would have to catch the young horses called foals.

The first sucessful capture of Przewalski's horses happened in 1899.

The plan had to be carried out in early spring. Then the foals would still be small. The hunters set out in the spring of 1897.

It was many days before they spotted a herd. The hunters trailed them for a long time before they could get close enough. They had to use their fastest riding horses to keep up with the Przewalski's horses.

Catching the Foals

The plan was to separate the foals from their mothers. The frightened foals would soon become too tired to run. Then the hunters could catch them with ropes.

The first year, the party caught a few foals. All of them died. The next spring, they caught six foals. They kept these foals alive longer by feeding them sheep's milk. But still, they all died within a few months.

A Successful Idea

Finally, someone had the idea to bring along domestic mares to feed the foals. The next year, in 1899, they caught seven foals. There were six female foals and one male. The mares' milk kept them alive. But the male and one female were too weak to travel. They were left at Assanov's home in Mongolia.

The other five females had to walk to the nearest train station. It was 300 miles (500 kilometers) away. Then they traveled another 3,000 miles (4,800 kilometers) by train. It took the foals almost a year to reach their new home.

The Przewalski's horse herd at Askania Nova numbers about 100 today.

Askania Nova

The next spring they all arrived safely at a train station in Ukraine. But the last leg of the trip was too much for one foal. She died on the trip from the station to Askania Nova. It was only 45 miles (70 kilometers) away. On March 1, 1900, four young Przewalski's mares finally reached the estate.

Meanwhile, the male that was left in Mongolia made a journey of his own. A Mongolian ruler bought him. The ruler gave the wild horse as a present to the czar (ZAHR) of Russia. Czar is what Russian kings were called until 1917. The male Przewalski's horse went to live at the czar's stable.

In 1904, the czar gave his Przewalski's horse to Askania Nova. This male became the first breeding stallion at the estate. A line of Przewalski's horses has lived at Askania Nova ever since. Today more Przewalski's horses live at Askania Nova than anywhere else in the world. The herd now numbers almost 100.

Askania Nova is an estate located in southern Ukraine. Askania Nova has had Przewalski's horses since their first capture. Today, it has more Przewalski's horses than anywhere else in the world.

Chapter 5

Zoos to the Rescue

By 1901, the hunting party was getting better at catching Przewalski's horses. They caught more than 50 live foals that year. Only 28 of them survived the months of travel across Asia. Twelve went to a private animal reserve in England. The rest were split up into pairs of one male and one female. They went to zoos in England, Germany, France, Holland, and the United States.

More foals were taken in 1902 and 1903. Some went to Askania Nova. Others ended up in zoos in the United States and Europe. A few captures took place in the 1930s and 1940s. But Przewalski's horses in the wild became

To help the Przewalski's horses survive, zoos started boarding them in the early 1900s.

harder and harder to find. The last Przewalski's horse taken from the wild was caught in 1947.

Extinct in the Wild

By the 1940s, Przewalski's horses were very rare. Only a few small groups were spotted once in a while. Most of these were killed in the 1950s. Some Mongolian soldiers found them on their way home from China. The soldiers were so hungry that they shot and ate the horses.

In 1966, the last Przewalski's horses were spotted in the Gobi Reserve in Mongolia. No one has seen a Przewalski's horse in the wild for more than 25 years. Without the foals born at Askania Nova and in the zoos, Przewalski's horses would be extinct.

The last Przewalski's horse was seen in the wild in the 1960s.

Chapter 6

Back to the Wild

Endangered species often begin to die out because their habitat disappears. An animal's habitat is the environment that is healthy for that animal. When their environment changes too much, the animals begin to have problems. That is what happened to Przewalski's horses.

Scientists and animal lovers saw this problem many years ago. The captured Przewalski's horses kept the breed alive. But they had to live in zoos or wildlife parks. If they had been released back into their natural habitat, they would have died.

But endangered species cannot last for a long time in zoos and parks. The breeding groups are too small. Animals that are too closely related cannot breed with each other.

The captured Przewalski's horses kept the breed alive.

Zoos must constantly trade animals to keep breeding possible. Traveling is hard on animals.

Restoring the Habitat

The best way to save an endangered species is to restore its habitat. Then people must help them return to the wild. It is not safe to release endangered animals into the wild in one big group. Bad weather or a natural disaster could kill all of them at one time. It is better to have a few smaller groups in separate regions.

The first Przewalski's horses returned to their native region in 1985. Eleven Przewalski's horses from England and Germany went to a zoo in western China. A year later, they were released into a wildlife park. They were still fenced in, but they had many acres to roam.

Home to Mongolia

June 5, 1992, was a special day in the history of Przewalski's horses. On that day, 16 Przewalski's horses walked off an airplane in Ulan Bator (OO-lahn Bah-TOUR), Mongolia.

The first Przewalski's horses returned to their native region in the Gobi Desert in 1985.

Dorsal Stripe

Zebra-Like Back

Tail

Lighter Undercoat

Eight were from Askania Nova, and eight were from a wildlife park in Holland.

The people of Mongolia celebrated the arrival of the takhi. Hundreds came to see the wild horses come off the plane. Some older people still remembered the herds of takhi on the steppe in days gone by.

Trucks took the animals to a nearby wildlife park. It is called Hustain Nuruu (Hohs-tah-EEN New-RUE) Reserve. Over the next few years, other Przewalski's horses from zoos around the world joined them.

Learning to be Free

The Przewalski's horses needed help when they first went into the wild. For a year or two, they stayed in a large fenced area. People made sure the horses found food and water. The horses were protected from hunters and wolves.

In the wild, all horses organize themselves into groups. Each group has a stallion for its leader. The other members of the group are mares and their foals. There are from five to 15 mares in each group.

Przewalski's horses organize themselves into groups in the wild. Each group has a stallion and several mares.

In June 1994, two groups went into the main reserve. Another group went free in July 1995. They live completely wild. Humans only check on them once in a while. Today there are about 200 Przewalski's horses running free in Mongolia.

Competing for Habitat

The Hustain Nuruu Reserve is in the middle of Mongolia's steppe region. Many farmers use this area to graze their cattle and sheep. In 1993 and 1994, the Mongolian government passed laws to protect Hustain Nuruu and the animals living in it. Now farmers must find other grasslands to feed their horses and cattle.

The people of Mongolia love the Przewalski's horse. It is part of their ancient past. Mongolians are working with zoo officials and animal lovers all over the world. They are trying to keep a place on the steppe for the Asian wild horse. They want to see the takhi run free again.

Mongolians call the Przewalski's horse takhi, which means spirit in their language.

Words to Know

dorsal stripe (DOHR-suhl stripe)—a stripe of differently colored hair running along an animal's backbone

dun (DUHN)—a tan color

endangered (en-DAYN-jurd)—in danger of becoming extinct

equine (EE-kwine)—an animal with qualities common to horses, donkeys, and zebras

extinct (ek-STINGKT)—no longer existing as a living animal or plant

foal (FOHL)—a young horse

forelock (FOHR-lok)—the part of a horse's mane that hangs down between the eyes like bangs

habitat (HAB-uh-tat)—the place or type of environment where a plant or animal naturally lives and grows

mare (MAIR)—a female horse

species (SPEE-sheez)—a class of animals having common traits, which normally breed only with each other

stallion (STAL-yuhn)—a male horse
steppe (STEHP)—a large region of open
grassland in Europe and Asia

To Learn More

Aldridge, James. *The Marvelous Mongolian*.
Boston: Little, Brown, 1974.

Boyd, Lee, and Katherine A. Houpt.
Przewalski's Horse. Albany, N.Y.: State
University of New York Press, 1994.

Clutton-Brock, Juliet. *Horse*. New York:
Alfred A. Knopf, 1992.

Edwards, Elwyn Hartley. *Encyclopedia of the
Horse*. New York: Dorling Kindersley, 1994.

You can read articles about Przewalski's
horses in the following magazines: *Equus*,
Horse and Pony, and *Riding*.

Useful Addresses

Foundation for the Preservation and Protection of the Przewalski's Horse
c/o Dr. Julia S. McCann
University of Georgia
322 Livestock-Poultry Building
Athens, GA 30602-2771
E-mail address: jmccann@uga.cc.uga.edu

International Museum of the Horse
4089 Iron Works Pike
Lexington, KY 40511-8434

Internet Sites

American Zoo and Aquarium Association
http://www.aza.org/aza/ssp/awhorse.html

Przewalski's Wild Horse
http://www.med.usf.edu/NINA/park/asian/horse.html

Takhi (The Mongolian Wild Horse)
http://www.halcyon.com/mongolia/Takhi.html

Takh: Society for the Przewalski's Horse
http://king.dom.de/takh/takh.html

Where to See Przewalski's Horses

Bronx Zoo/Wildlife Conservation Park
New York, New York

Calgary Zoo
Calgary, Alberta, Canada

Denver Zoological Gardens
Denver, Colorado

Detroit Zoological Institute
Royal Oak, Michigan

Gladys Porter Zoo
Brownsville, Texas

Metropolitan Toronto Zoo
Toronto, Ontario, Canada

Minnesota Zoo
Apple Valley, Minnesota

Northeast Nebraska Zoo
Royal, Nebraska

San Diego Wild Animal Park
Escondido, California

The Wilds
Cumberland, Ohio

Index

Askania Nova, 24, 28-29, 31, 40

Assanov, Nikolai, 24-25, 27

Büchner, C.E., 24

cave, 7-8

China, 23, 33, 37

Clemenz, D.A., 24

czar, 29

donkey, 11, 13

dorsal stripe, 13

endangered species, 5, 35, 37

environment, 35

equine, 11

extinct, 7, 33

Falz-Fein, Friederich von, 24-25

forelock, 15

Gobi Desert, 21

Gobi Reserve, 33

Grum-Grzhimailo, Grigory and Mikhail, 23-24

habitat, 35, 37, 43

height, 4, 15

hunt, 9, 19, 23-27, 31, 40

Hustain Nuruu Reserve, 40, 43

Khan, Genghis, 9

Lascaux, France, 7

Manchuria, 9

mane, 4, 13

Mongolia, 5, 8-9, 20-21, 23-25, 27, 29, 33, 37, 40, 43

Poliakov, Dr. I.S., 21

Przewalski, Nikolai, 19-21, 23-24

species, 4-5, 21, 24, 35

steppe, 17, 19, 40, 43

St. Petersburg, 21, 24

Takhin Shar Nuruu, 20-21

takhi, 21, 40, 43

Tibet, 8

Ukraine, 24, 28-29

Ulan Bator, Mongolia, 37

weight, 4, 15

wildlife park, 5, 9, 35, 37, 40

zebra, 11, 15

zoo, 5, 9, 31, 33, 37, 40, 43